Dedicated to my niece, Laura,
who prays for Bo, her dog, her family
and friends . . . and all their pets.

Introduction

Anyone who has ever had a dog knows dogs give unconditional love. It occurred to me that maybe they're here to show us how.

What if someone loved me like my beautiful, precious collie, Lady? She was a warm, wagging, wriggling golden fuzz ball given to me by my father on my fourteenth Christmas. When I pulled off the bow and opened her box, she whined eagerly, sprinkled my face with delicate, dry puppy kisses, and took over my body as her personal playground. There was only one thing to do about Lady. I promptly fell in love with her.

Then there was a call when I was away at school that she had died suddenly from a heart attack, and part of me died, too. But *how she loved* is still with me, and if it ever walked into my life on two legs, I'd be the happiest person on earth.

Wouldn't you, if someone loved you like your dog?

– B.F.

Could You Love Me Like My Dog?

BETH FOWLER

A FIRESIDE BOOK PUBLISHED BY SIMON & SCHUSTER INC.

NEW YORK LONDON TORONTO SYDNEY TOKYO SINGAPORE

FIRESIDE
Rockefeller Center
1230 Avenue of the Americas
New York, New York 10020

Copyright © 1996 by Beth Fowler

All rights reserved, including the right of reproduction in whole or in part in any form.

FIRESIDE and colophon are registered trademarks of Simon & Schuster Inc.

Designed & illustrated by Jill Weber

Manufactured in the United States of America

10 9 8 7 6 5 4 3 2 1

Library of Congress Cataloging-in-Publication Data is available.

ISBN 0-684-81900-7

Beth Fowler is the owner of the trademarks
"COULD YOU LOVE ME LIKE MY™" and "I WOOF YOU™"

Special thanks to those who made this possible:

*my family, Janet, Greg, Louise, Hazel, Vi, Carol, Jan, Mary Anne, Linda,
Anne, Kelly, Julie, Mairead, Megan, Michelle, Mack, Aaron, Dan, David,
Laurie, Mark, Carolyn, Richard, John, and Steve.*

Could you smother me with kisses
each time I enter the room, even though
I've only been gone for thirty seconds?

Could you always think I look great, no matter what I have on?

Could you savor whatever I put in front of you, even though it's straight from the can?

Could you forgive anything and never hold a grudge, especially when it's my fault?

8

Could you never have a bad day?

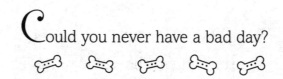

Could you like my dirty clothes
and smelly gym shoes, the dirtier
and smellier the better?

Could you not mind when
I say you have death breath?

11

Could you be interested in meeting new people, but always come back to me?

Could you pant for me?

13

Could you take it in stride
when I pull your nose out of
other people's business?

14

Could you lick my toes?

Could you always bump
into doorways and walls in
your rush to greet me?

Could you like it when I grab your tail?

Could you always be nice
to my friends and family?

Could you not care if people stare when you're doing leg lifts?

19

Could you just spit it out if
there's something you don't like?

Could you be sorry if you bark at me?

Could you always be thrilled to go on a drive or an errand, as long as it's with me?

Could you follow me anywhere?

Could you announce it's bedtime
with huge yawns that squeak at
the end?

Could you never stop
heavy-breathing in my ear?

Could you hunt around for what's new to do and see?

Could you leave when I say it's time to go home?

Could you never change how you feel about me?

Could you whimper and whine
when we're apart?

Could you entertain me when you sleep by snorting and pawing the air?

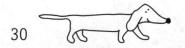

Could you always nuzzle my neck?

31

Could you warn the whole neighborhood when things go bump in the night?

Could you always protect me?

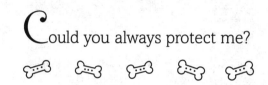

Could you prowl the streets
and alleys for something unusual
to bring home?

🦴 🦴 🦴 🦴 🦴

Could you always curl up beside me?

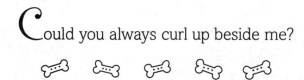

Could you never stop putting
your head in my lap?

Could you always be the same little puppy inside, even when you're old and gray?

Could you jump me within two
seconds of when I walk in the door?

Could you always keep me warm?

Could you let me read the newspaper before you tear into it?

Could you always wake me up
with a kiss?

Could you point out interesting people and things, even if you have to drag me over to see them?

🦴 🦴 🦴 🦴 🦴

Could you never criticize me?

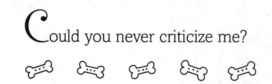

Could you work out my arms as well as my legs every time we go for a walk?

Could you worship the Frisbee?

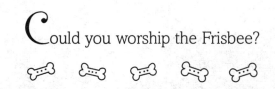

Could you never hesitate to ask for seconds?

🦴 🦴 🦴 🦴 🦴

Could you stop if I restrain you?

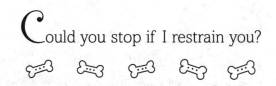

Could you answer the door prepared to defend me from strangers and people in uniforms?

🦴 🦴 🦴 🦴 🦴

Could you feel okay if you lose some hair?

Could you love the smell of my hair, my hands, my clothes, my ears . . . my any- and everything?

Could you bury and forget any bones I pick with you?

Could you always be happy with what you have?

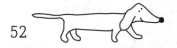

Could you never complain?

Could you eat red meat and
not be too dainty to pick it up
and gnaw the bone?

Could you always take my side?

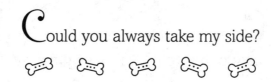

Could you understand my moods
and not blame me for having them?

Could you never bite my head off?

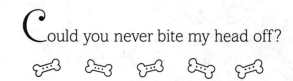

Could you show how much you like the furniture by jumping and climbing all over it?

Could you always be gentle and sweet to children?

Could you always do your best?

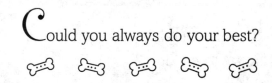

Could you go to the curb when
I say "on your mark, get set, go"?

🦴 🦴 🦴 🦴 🦴

Could you lie down with me by
the fire?

Could you not mind feeling chained to me?

Could you stand it if I tied you up
with bristly rope instead of satin?

Could you give me little tiny
love nips when you get excited?

Could you stay when I ask?

Could you always let me know
where you are by sprawling
full-length on the floor?

Could you never wag your paw at me?

🦴 🦴 🦴 🦴 🦴

Could you always wag your tail?

Could you wonder at the beauty of
every stick and rock and squirrel?

Could you be eager to have a ball?

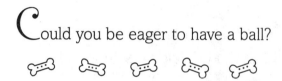

71

Could you like my cooking enough
to slurp and gulp your food?

Could you always keep a secret?

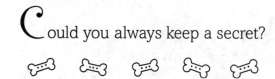

Could you take a whiff and tickle the backs of my knees?

Could you nibble my fingers?

Could you never get mad at me,
even when I'm yanking your chain?

Could you accept it when I say "no"?

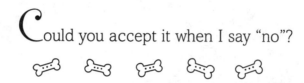

Could you grin and wiggle your
ears when I say your name?

Could you always listen and hang on my every word?

Could you sniff out new trails
that are off the beaten path?

Could you find your way back to me, even if you were lost?

81

Could your eyes always shine at me with love and acceptance?

🦴 🦴 🦴 🦴 🦴

Could you be my best friend and constant companion?

Could you never be embarrassed
by public displays of affection?

Could you always enjoy petting?

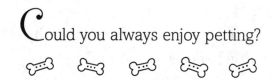

Could you tap dance through the door whenever we go out?

Could you help clean out the refrigerator?

Could you shake hands and speak when you're introduced?

Could you not take it personally
when I ask you to be quiet?

Could you share my love of the great outdoors?

Could you celebrate each spring by helping me dig up all the flowerbeds ?

Could you quiver with happiness
just being near me?

Could you not mind when I push
you away because you're drooling?

Could you let me dress you up
and take silly photos just because
they make me smile?

Could you cherish the little presents I give you, like used tennis balls and worn-out socks?

Could you tolerate me keeping you on a short leash whenever we're in public?

Could you never growl or snap at me?

Could you give up your favorite chair for me?

Could you beg for my attention?

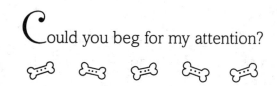

Could you love to drive with the windows down and feel the wind in your face?

Could you always point the way?

Could you help me with the dishes and polish off the leftovers?

Could you time your bathroom stops so they fit my schedule?

Could you always be ready for a great roll in the dirt or the leaves . . . or the hay?

Could you always be there?

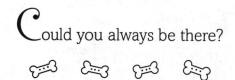

Could you conserve towels
by shaking dry?

Could you always be ready to play?

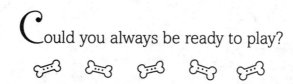

Could you yelp for joy at
the sound of my footsteps?

Could you let me run my fingers
through your hair?

Could you suffer through bubble baths because I love how they make you smell?

Could you never become a yapper?

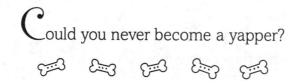

Could you leap tall tables in a single bound to personally deliver the mail?

Could you always chase me?

Could you put me first in your life before the newspaper or any outside interests?

Could you always understand?

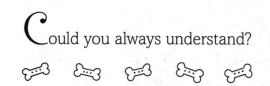

Could you not mind if there's not a clean glass and you have to drink from the faucet?

116

Could you help water the grass?

Could you control your killer instinct even when it's brought on by insufferable cattiness?

Could you flop down and relax in any situation?

Could you bound up in ecstasy
when my car turns in to the driveway?

120

Could you clean up any
spills on the kitchen floor?

Could you never have trouble
rolling over and going to sleep?

Could you not snarl when
I tickle your feet?

Could you be a beach bum and chase the waves with me?

Could you cut loose and howl
at the moon?

Could you always shudder on the way to see the doctor?

Could you trust me?

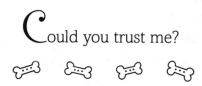

Could you try not to make big messes for me to clean up?

Could you never worry?

129

Could you help me get out of bed each morning by slowly pulling off the covers?

Could you never intentionally scratch me with your toenails?

Could you get a haircut when you're looking a little shaggy?

Could you empty the trash?

Could you jump through hoops for me?

🦴 🦴 🦴 🦴 🦴

Could you always care?

Could you never expect expensive gifts?

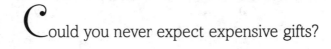

Could you always be kind?

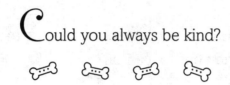

Could you always have a warm shoulder to lean on?

🦴 🦴 🦴 🦴 🦴

Could you help me up when I fall?

Could you be content if I fenced you in?

Could you be patient?

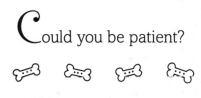

Could you not be self-conscious
about your body?

Could you be a connoisseur of water-tasting from puddles and creeks and pools?

Could you slink along with your belly on the floor whenever you're in the doghouse?

Could you never chew me out?

Could you catch whatever I toss
your way?

Could you never stop pawing me?

Could you leave a little trail of footprints so I never have to wonder where you went?

Could you share your favorite things with me?

Could you never be embarrassed
when nature calls?

Could you make a splash
wherever you go?

Could you be so comfortable with
me that sometimes you just doze off?

Could you always track down anything?

Could you love it when the sink leaks and you get to mop it up yourself?

Could you always have a hot body?

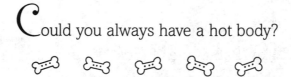

Could you answer to pet names like "Baby" and "Precious" and not think they sound ridiculous?

Could you lap my sweat?

Could you take everything
I say seriously?

Could you always be loyal?

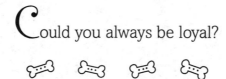

159

Could you dedicate your life to me?